THE POLAR ESCAPADE

A Journey To A New Beginning

Vivvaan Bajpayee

Published by Bookosmia, 2024

First Printing, 2024
Edited by Sowmya Rajendran
Cover art by Bhavana D

ISBN 978-93-6045-746-4

Printed at Thomson Press (India) Ltd

*To my little brother Rihaan,
who wanted to hear a bedtime story
about polar bears travelling, and
that's how this story evolved!*

PREFACE

What is climate change?

A child in Mumbai is at a hospital. He cries to his mother, "My chest is feeling tight. I can't breathe."

A tourist guide in Kashmir worries that there will be no snow and no tourists.

A monkey thinks of moving away as the trees in the jungle are now being chopped down for wood like his earlier dwelling.

A bird weeps over not finding food before it is shot by a hunter in the jungle.

Trees swirl in the breeze before they are razed to the ground by acid rain and chopped for wood.

The tide swells with the glaciers that have given rise to an angry ocean.

In the city, air conditioning to avoid the 40-degree weather is prevalent. Yet it just worsens things.

Black, wormy oil spills into the river, killing the fish and spoiling the water that people bathe in and drink.

Migratory birds have no living space, and they cannot migrate. Most of them die from lack of food and the harsh weather.

Polar bears lose their habitat to the melting of ice across the Arctic. The loss of seals also causes them to lose a staple food.

To make the human race unstoppable, automobiles fly across the streets, leaving behind a trail of smoke. This causes skyrocketing temperatures.

This is Climate Change.

Only we can fight it.

- Vivvaan Bajpayee

CRISIS ACROSS THE ARCTIC
ARCTIC
CRACK
CRACK!!
THE PLAN
THE JOURNEY
GREENLAND
NUUK GOVT.

CONTENTS

PROLOGUE

21st June 1776

"One of the children in thy bloodline,
will be the greatest saviour of nature in all time."

The prophecy reverberated in the ears of Miko the Crusader as he stumbled out of the cave. Fragments of memory, the flash of the Oracle and the hollow scream of the phoenix as it was reduced to ash.

Everything had gone wrong, or was it right?

Like ripples shattering the smooth surface of the water, disturbing dreams woke him from his sleep. The prophecy plagued him day and night subconsciously, a feeling he could not comprehend. But he knew the emotional tremors were deep; he braced for an impact he could not yet predict.

A part of him was dumbfounded, refusing to believe what he had heard.

He recalled the moments of the last few days when he had arrived at the Oracle's cave.

* * *

Miko the Crusader dragged his feet.

Though a polar bear, he was rather frozen. He felt like he was trapped in a block of ice. The icy wind blew in a blizzard, making every step of his journey slower. Boulders of blue ice and glaciers; slippery blocks that just increased the difficulty of his journey – the journey across the Arctic. But he needed to consult the Oracle.

The Oracle lay ahead in the icicle-strewn caves. The cavern pulsated with energy. An eerie glow burned his eyes.

The Oracle was once a rare metallic rock that transformed into a ball of energy. It was struck by the force of the 1556 earthquake. It had the greatest power on Earth – the power to answer any question.

In 1598, Miko's forefather Horatio the Helpful had approached the Oracle in the quest for a suitable place to move to, a place that would be appropriate for his clan to live. As the human race swelled and took over more and more areas, he knew he would have to move away to a distant place with hospitable conditions. The Oracle told him to move further north, towards the poles.

In 1699, his great grandfather Meccus the Explorer, had found the way to the Arctic, based on the coordinates

provided by the Oracle. He brought the Oracle with him to the Arctic.

The Oracle could be contacted very rarely and mostly only by the ancient polar bears. Then, a torrent of lightning bolts had defibrillated the Oracle, and now, anyone could approach it.

Only during emergencies, that is.
Miko knew that this was an emergency.

The moment his cubs were born, he was supposed to leave them. It was what all fathers did in the polar bear bloodline. Instead, he could only gaze in awe as the light in the Arctic drained for a minute.

It felt like a bone-chilling polar night, but on the summer solstice.

With a swoosh, a phoenix – a messenger of the Oracle – swooped into the cave, illuminating it. “Visit the Oracle!” hollered the phoenix, before it burst into flames, the fire illuminating the Arctic once again.

An ancient sign.

A sign that their bloodline would achieve greatness. But of what kind?

That was a story untold.

Miko hauled himself inside and whispered the words – “Oracle of light, Oracle of bay. Show me the truth, as clear as day.”

The hardened cube of light blue ice burned yellow hot and blasted itself into sheets and pellets of frozen rain. When the ice parted, it left behind a dark green orb. The orb flared up and an ancient voice – the voice of Socrates, the philosopher – roared – "Speak, O great one!"

Miko whispered, "Why did an ancient symbol appear when my children were born?" The orb burned dark purple.

It whispered a message of hope.

The orb hit the ice and cratered it. It would soon freeze back for the next asker. Miko collapsed on the floor. He couldn't breathe.

The Oracle's words echoed in his ears.

"They'll risk their lives for a treasure
That holds no measure."

254 years later…

2030: The year of global warming

Hope is distant.

Fear rules, every part of the world is tingling with it.

Disaster is knocking at the Earth's door.

The north and south poles whip up powerful winds.

A force, menacingly residing in the air, melts ice into water.

A cry rings out, but no one hears it.

This is the story of two polar bears, desperate to rescue their clan and save their home, come what may…

* * *

"One of the children in thy bloodline
will be the greatest saviour of nature in all time."

CHAPTER

I

The Abode Of The Ice Hunters

The ice hunters of the Arctic
In this world so chaotic!

The sky awoke with morning's birth. The sun exploded onto the world. But, only a thin ray of light shone through the Arctic Circle, thawing the ice, and radiating hope in the bitter cold of the winter.

Little did the polar bears know that this hope was their North Star.

It was winter, and yes, it was cold, no doubt. However, unlike other places in the world, here, the Earth tilted itself away from the sun, and sunlight was not seen for a stretch of six months. It was as though the Earth was at war with the sun.

Rahul stretched himself on the ice. In the winters, he felt — oh so very sleepy — but, he rose, for he had a duty to fend for his younger brother, Amar.

Amar lay asleep in the cave, which was a bunker of ice. Rahul ventured out, looking for trickles of water.

The Arctic was cold, but global warming caused by humans had melted many of the thick glaciers. So, he went, pawprints crunching over the ice. He finally sighted a thin line of water.

NO FISH. HE GRUNTED.

The fish population had been decimated, and squabbles among the bears had begun to break out for food. If a bear spotted a fish, he ought not to let it go, for his family would starve that day.

In the last decade, the Arctic foxes and seals had vanished from the land. Ice had gradually given way to water, and the sea level was growing higher.

The fog was rising high above their heads, making it difficult to breathe though their lungs had adapted to the polar gales which blew aplenty in the Northern areas.

Rahul stuck his snout inside the water and waited for the fish to approach. He would spot their shadows moving underwater before he saw them.

He waited and waited. No shadow.

He was about to stick his snout in again when a ripple went through the water. He lunged at the fish and after waving it about for a while, it stopped wriggling.

A PRIZE!

He dragged it back to the cave.

For he was a polar bear, with his majestic white fur gleaming under the sky.

"One of the children in thy bloodline
will be the greatest saviour of nature in all time.
They'll risk their lives for a treasure
That holds no measure."

CHAPTER

II

The Polar Bear Family

A snuggly home for polar bears
Grandparents tell them stories of battles and dares.

The polar bear family consisted of Rahul, Amar, their parents, Grandma and Grandpa Bear.

Apart from this circle, they also mingled with the other polar bears in the Arctic. Once, they abounded in the Arctic, but not anymore, as food had become meagre.

When cubs were born, parents in the clan would wonder "Are these the polar bears who will fulfil the prophecy?" So, they would always contact the Oracle. When Rahul and Amar were born, their parents approached the Oracle too, hoping for suitable names that would reflect their wit and power. The Oracle named them so, as Rahul's name meant

‘**Conqueror of all miseries**’ and Amar’s name meant ‘**Immortal**’.

Their parents looked after them very well. They brought them meals, played with them, and taught them how to keep the humans in the frigid Arctic at bay, though they seemed to be evacuating nearly every day. The polar bears never fought the humans: it was as though a pact had made them stay away from people.

Their grandparents used to tell them stories galore.
Their stories about the Arctic before it was so polluted.

When the fish were abundant, they could poke a snout in the water and come out with two whoppers. When the ice was a proper terrain.

The icebergs were not so light and fragile then, and they used to jump and skip and prance and rollick all over the ice without fear that they would end up at the bottom of the Arctic Ocean.

They also told them legendary stories of polar bears who sought out quests and changed the lives of everyone in the Arctic.

They told them stories of brave polar bears who went on glorious crusades to save and protect, ancestors whose names were engraved in history.

Rahul and Amar enjoyed ‘story hour’ the best and longed to be like their forefathers and foremothers.

Over the years, polar bears had learned the human language. When humans came to the Arctic, the polar bears’ ability to talk to them ensured that there was no conflict.

"One of the children in thy bloodline
will be the greatest saviour of nature in all time.
They'll risk their lives for a treasure
That holds no measure.
Sailing across the clear blue sky
Simply on a gay whim, their spirits high!"

CHAPTER

III

Crisis Across The Arctic

Amar wants to voyage,
However, the ice is in the melting stage!

Rahul brought the fish back home and after a meagre yet delicious meal, the brothers wandered out. The other polar bears in the vicinity kept away.

Rahul could look quite ferocious when he wanted. Amar enjoyed his brother's protection. As they strolled around, they paused to admire the gleaming sun on the horizon.

"I want to see the world outside," said Amar.

"We'll see it one day," said Rahul. He wasn't sure whether they would ever set foot outside the Arctic.

But why not?

There were many polar bears who had gone to other places. Over the years, several friendly faces, like Tarun, Ashish and Susie had been whisked to many places outside the Arctic. They were put to sleep and carried by huge flying birds.

Tarun had been taken to the Singapore Zoo.
Ashish had been taken to the North Pole exhibit in Canada.
Susie had been taken to Malaysia.

Rahul pondered the uncertainties of life outside the Arctic. The polar bears taken to zoos and enclosures were not allowed to hunt and live the way they did in the wild. At the zoos, they would have the surety of fish, but in a cage. The world outside the Arctic was warming fast too!

It was a misery that all the polar bears who were captured faced. Eventually, their health deteriorated and they were dropped back at the Arctic, sighing with relief that their ordeal was over.

No! You always say that! I really want to go!" said Amar, stomping his foot. Rahul stared at his brother and opened his mouth to say something when…

CRA-ACK!

Rahul and Amar looked down to see the ice splintering. They were on either side of the crack, which could prove to be fatal.

Rahul remembered what his mother had told him about ice cracks.

"It means that the ice is going to break," she had told him.

A nanosecond before the ice parted, Amar hopped onto his brother's back, and Rahul flung himself on an iceberg. They watched as the ice tumbled to the bottom of the abysmal water.

Several chunks of icebergs, also termed growlers or bergy bits, were seen floating all around the place. The ice had disappeared off the face of the Earth and Amar and Rahul had barely survived. The small growlers were the only sign of the existence of the ice.

"One of the children in thy bloodline
will be the greatest saviour of nature in all time.
They'll risk their lives for a treasure
That holds no measure.
Sailing across the clear blue sky
Simply on a gay whim, their spirits high!
To find inner calling, despite beration;
Unflinching against the greater conflagration."

CHAPTER IV

Susie's Homecoming

Humans in helicopters raise a noisy storming
While Susie tells everyone about global warming.

As the next fortnight passed, many such cracks and melting of the ice were seen.

Polar bears all but disappeared, and many familiar faces were lost.

A few of them, including Rahul and Amar, stayed in their caves, for they, apart from the extreme weather conditions, had never faced anything too bad yet.

Silence ruled the Arctic until one day, a noise was heard in the sky.

CHKA – CHKA – CHKA – CHKA

To those who had not seen the machine before, it looked like a strange bird. To their horror, it started to land on the ice! The polar bears who had visited places outside the Arctic knew that it was a helicopter.

Rahul and Tarun were confused! Why was it here again? The polar bears lowed and bayed and growled, to no avail.

As it came closer, they saw a huge net dangling from the helicopter. It had a polar bear strapped to it! Tarun could vaguely recollect how he was brought back home. He remembered having a lavish meal in Singapore zoo one day and when he woke up later, he found himself amidst friends at home, in the Arctic.

The helicopter was lowered onto the ice. The humans stepped out, untied the knots and released the bear.

Gradually, the polar bear woke from its slumber. All of them recognised it as their friend Susie.

Susie had been taken as an exhibit of the North Pole to Malaysia. She was the smartest of them and had been long gone. But she couldn't adapt to the habitat, and based on the veterinary doctor's recommendation, Susie was brought back.

The bears gave her a hearty welcome. They stood on their hind legs and roared a friendly greeting. They rushed towards her and nuzzled her. She was a close friend of theirs, and they had felt terrible when she was taken away.

The polar bears shared their woes. It was a relief to talk to someone so friendly and intelligent, someone who had interacted with humans. Perhaps she could find a solution.

Susie described life in the much warmer place she had been to. Luckily, she had had snow in her exhibit. The humans would often come and point fingers, scream loudly, take pictures with some slabs that they held all the time. It was so annoying!

Susie was thinking of speaking to them, but she was afraid that she would come to harm. She was gawked at to no end. But luckily, the Smartypants, as usual, had learned a great deal.

Susie said, "I just made an important discovery! When I was in the zoo in Malaysia, I found out why our icebergs break and crumble! Do you know that humans have special towers which squirt smoke? They heat our cold icebergs and make them melt.

On my way here, I saw the B 31 iceberg melting! They called it **GOBLAL WARNING...OR GOBAL WARMING...OR...**"

"**GLOBAL WARMING?**" suggested Tarun.

"Yes!" said Susie.

At that very moment, a thunderous crack was heard and it drew many yells from the humans.

They whirled around, only to see that the ice had given way, and that the humans were floundering in the water.

The huge helicopter had broken into two pieces! "You see what I mean," said Susie.

All the polar bears fled for their homes at once. Soon, only Rahul and Amar were left standing there.

"What do we do?" cried Amar.

Rahul turned to him wide-eyed and said, "We might have to leave the Arctic as soon as we can."

Amar was worried about this. He wanted to travel, but since the Arctic was falling to bits, was it really safe to do so?

Rahul reassured him and told him not to worry. They were going to go to a special place which had a human population. And yet, it would be cooler than a normal human habitat.

Their mother had explained the geography of the Arctic well to him. Rahul traced a small map of the nearby countries.

His paw came to rest on the southern part of a country called Greenland. Its capital. And that was where they were going.

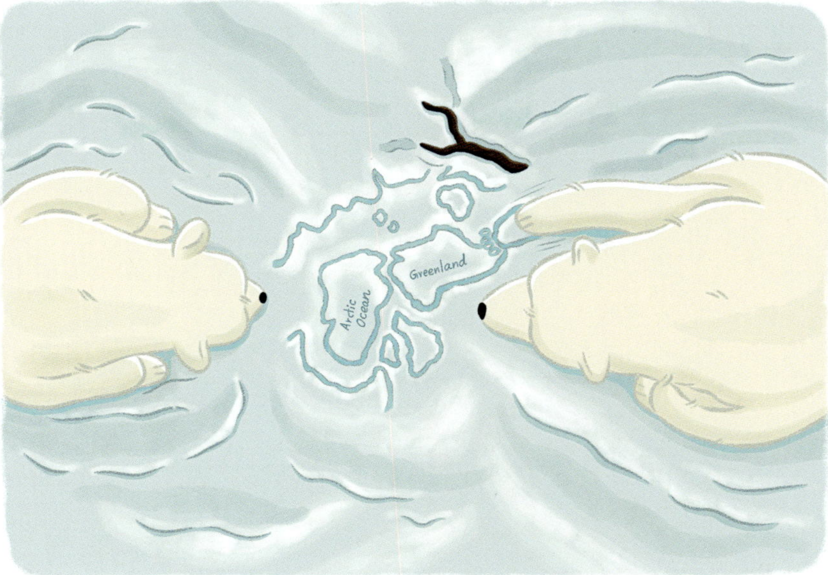

His mother said they had some connection to Greenland, though they did not know what. Maybe their ancestors had lived there once? No time to dig into the past. All eyes had to be on the future. They had to reach Greenland as fast as possible.

"One of the children in thy bloodline
will be the greatest saviour of nature in all time.
They'll risk their lives for a treasure
That holds no measure.
Sailing across the clear blue sky
Simply on a gay whim, their spirits high!
To find inner calling, despite beration;
Unflinching against the greater conflagration.
A world plundered by humans – What will they do?
Renew this periled world anew."

CHAPTER

V

The Journey And The Steamer Attack

On the borders of the coastline, they are stuck,
Until a steamer arrives and smashes ice, so duck!

Rahul stood outside the cave, tapping his paws impatiently. Amar was yet to wake up. When instructed to do so, he had just given the classic sleep excuse — five more minutes.

However, the five minutes had stretched to 10!

"Amar, get up!" he said, shaking his little brother.

"Please give me five minutes more!" replied a half-awake Amar.

"No! Get up now Amar! Or we won't go to Greenland!" Rahul scolded him.

At the mention of Greenland, Amar was up in three seconds flat. With just a couple of codfish in hand, Rahul and Amar set off for Greenland.

It was a long walk.

After a few days, Amar became tired and wanted to rest. They had walked and swum for a long time now. They ate the food that they had packed. When they set off again, they walked and swam, and walked and swam for three days, until they reached a coastline along the Arctic Ocean.

Here they dropped down and fell asleep. They fished and had a grand meal, of course, they did. But how would they possibly get to Greenland? There were huge crowds of humans coming to the Arctic, but they only came by plane or ship. How would they get across?

They had never seen so many fish in their life, in the Arctic Circle. They were taking a siesta when they heard a loud, blaring noise. Startled, they looked up to see a huge steamer approaching fast. It was going to crash against one of the large glaciers! The polar bears took to their heels and at the last moment, threw themselves on the smooth ice.

Chunks and boulders of blue ice and hardened glaciers which had frozen for countless millennia now splintered at the first hit by the humans.

The chunks flew high up in the air, casting a shadow on the surface. When they came crashing down, ice smashing against ice, huge craters were created in the glaciers.

Cracks flew fast across the surface and at least 500 metres of ice disappeared under the water. Rahul and Amar were horrified as they experienced firsthand the damage that could be done by the humans.

"One of the children in thy bloodline
will be the greatest saviour of nature in all time.
They'll risk their lives for a treasure
That holds no measure.
Sailing across the clear blue sky
Simply on a gay whim, their spirits high!
To find inner calling, despite beration;
Unflinching against the greater conflagration.
A world plundered by humans – What will they do?
Renew this periled world anew.
Touch the blackening sky from afar
To find the environmental lodestar."

CHAPTER

VI

The HDMS Nautilus Crusade

Are humans ready to lend a hand?
Polar bears yell, "Here we come, Greenland!"

The steamer lowered a ramp and a few men walked out. These men were strong and tempted the polar bears with fish. The polar bears growled but hesitated. At that very moment, the men quickly tossed the fish into their mouths. After eating it, they felt woozy, and lost their balance.

"This trick always works," said one man to another, as they hustled the polar bears aboard.

The polar bears were worried. They wanted to flee, attack, and do something to protect themselves. However, at the same time, they felt helpless and shook with fear.

The men, all dressed alike, took the polar bears aboard and showed them to the captain.

The captain gave a huge grin and said, "Good work, team. A pair of fully grown polar bears so fast. I knew having an icebreaker ship would work. We made it so quickly! We can drop them off at the checkpoint." He turned to a man and asked, "At which harbour are the polar bears supposed to be dropped off?"

The radio officer replied, "We can drop them off at Nuuk Port. Greenland's the drop–off, after all. Also good for their survival. It's cold and Greenland also has the least amount of pollution." With that, he stared down at the polar bears intently.

GREENLAND!

"What a stroke of luck!" thought Rahul.

The polar bears, over time, learnt that this steamer, with two forty-horsepower diesel engines, was here to evacuate the North Pole and take the inhabitants to safer locations. However, it was an icebreaker ship and smashed ice to bits. This, they felt, was unnecessary destruction. The Arctic was rapidly losing its wildlife and it was not safe for an endangered species like their own here.

A secluded area of the deck was reserved for their meals. A few more polar bears were there, but they mostly ignored Amar and Rahul. By instinct, they did not trust the men, but they desperately needed to get to Greenland.

The men often made jokes at their expense. A man pointed a stick at Rahul and asked, "Hey, where do you live?"

Rahul found himself responding with ease: "I live in the Arctic, Sir!" The men stared in shock, and Rahul felt pleased that he had spoken to a human being.

After that, the men feared the bears too and distanced themselves as much as they could.

They were tossed some salmon by the moustachioed Captain.

After a long and hearty meal, they fell asleep under the star-filled sky.

"One of the children in thy bloodline
will be the greatest saviour of nature in all time.
They'll risk their lives for a treasure
That holds no measure.
Sailing across the clear blue sky
Simply on a gay whim, their spirits high!
To find inner calling, despite beration;
Unflinching against the greater conflagration.
A world plundered by humans – What will they do?
Renew this periled world anew.
Touch the blackening sky from afar
To find the environmental lodestar.
Feel the cruel feats of man
Find solace within their plan."

CHAPTER

VIII

Greenland, At Last!

Greenland — an absolute paradise
Where they speak to people to help save the ice.

The loud blaring of the steamer shook them awake from their sleep. It was racing to the shores.

WHOOOOO! WHOOOOOO!

They took a look at the town they were approaching. It had snow-covered mountains and houses of red, turquoise, and yellow. The roads were snow-covered too, with mountain alder trees.

The people were walking slowly throughout the lanes and paths. The roofs of houses and pavements were white from the snow.

Their first view of Greenland would stay in their minds forever.

The captain was shunting the other polar bears from the ship into cages. Rahul and Amar had to get away from the men!

They quickly dived off the edge of the ship and into the cold ocean. A due bit of yelling was heard, yet the polar bears managed to swim to the shore and run away, across the streets. What with the snow matching their fur, it was almost as if they had vanished into thin air.

They passed by a dramatic-looking man with a strange expression – he was afraid of them and began to run. But Amar nuzzled him and said, "Don't worry, we won't attack you. We have never attacked a human and we never will!"

The man was moved and signalled his friend to join him. His friend, who had been watching the scene unfold from a distance, came closer and said, “Where do you wander little bears?”

“We are from the Arctic. We have lost our home.”

“It is a pity. Well, welcome to Nuuk. Why don’t you ask somebody to help you out with the problem in your home?”

This was an excellent idea! But whom would they talk to?

The polar bears wandered around, frightened by the tourists and tour guides. They walked amidst people wearing thick parkas, mittens, and thick black leather boots.

They wandered away from laughing kids making snowmen and sculptures of bears, deer and a few dogs.

They did not know where to go or what to do as Greenland was quite different from the other cities about which they had heard.

Polar bears who had been outside the Arctic had described cities as places with lots of cars, taxis, buses and huge skyscrapers, inhabited by people speaking different languages. Here, all the humans spoke Greenlandic like the man they had seen earlier. They were glued to gadgets that Susie described as ‘Silly Slabs’.

While they were soaking in the serene beauty of Greenland, their attention was grabbed by a noisy truck that was approaching them.

As they gazed on, they saw a man in a black suit step down from the truck. He had an air of authority about him. This government official was instructing the men to thaw the ice by sprinkling salt on the roads.

They had a hunch that this man could help them.

They went up to the man and asked him for help. They murmured in his ears, "We are from the Arctic Circle. Icebergs in the Arctic are melting and breaking apart. Our clan is in danger. We may not have a home to go back to. Our forefathers predicted that our clan would be wiped out by 2100. We need some help in saving all the polar bears." Once again, Rahul managed to speak to the humans, and Amar joined in, adding a few lines in broken human language.

The man was startled to hear this. He knew some polar bears were coming to Greenland, but he had never imagined that they would be chatting with him. They were to be released in a nearby reserve, not in the open streets! However, he was also deeply touched by their story. This kind-hearted man took them to an office that was surrounded by armed men and authorization check posts.

An armed man grinned and said jokingly, “Paramilitary or polar military?”

This man was authorised to go in with the polar bears.

He went near the door and asked the polar bears, “You are about to meet the most powerful person in the country. Are you ready?”

The polar bears took a deep breath.

They braced themselves for an encounter they would never forget.

"One of the children in thy bloodline
will be the greatest saviour of nature in all time.
They'll risk their lives for a treasure
That holds no measure.
Sailing across the clear blue sky
Simply on a gay whim, their spirits high!
To find inner calling, despite beration;
Unflinching against the greater conflagration.
A world plundered by humans – What will they do?
Renew this periled world anew.
Touch the blackening sky from afar
To find the environmental lodestar.
Feel the cruel feats of man
Find solace within their plan.
Walk across accursed land,
Yet, beauty lies within hand."

CHAPTER VIII

The Confrontation

To the prime minister's office, they go
Problems of global warming, they show.

As they walked into a large room, they observed a man at a desk with a nameplate, whom they later came to know was the Prime Minister of Greenland.

Amar was afraid as there were also many people with cameras, reporters and journalists listening, recording, and scribbling on pads and notebooks.

A camerawoman was filming the Prime Minister's opinions on 'Global Warming' and the 'Arctic evacuation'.

A lady exclaimed in a loud, bold, and dramatic voice – "As the Prime Minister confirms, many of the polar bears have been evacuated from the Arctic and oh! What a surprise, look where two of them have turned up!"

All the cameras turned towards Rahul and Amar, and they were flabbergasted and anxious at the same time.

The man who had led them there whispered something into the Prime Minister's ear while there was pin-drop silence in the room.

The Prime Minister moved closer to Rahul and Amar.

He asked them many questions:

"What are your names?"

"I am Amar and he is Rahul. We are brothers," Amar responded quickly.

"Are you from the Arctic? Were you evacuated recently?" asked the PM.

"Yes, my forefathers hailed from the Arctic. They initially were in a region south of the Arctic, but after a few thousand years, they shifted to the Arctic. My forefathers had discovered the Arctic and built our homes though ours is one of the last clans to reach the Arctic," replied Rahul. He was well informed of their history.

"Being a personal witness and victim to this grave situation, can you describe the problem for all of us here?" interrogated the PM.

"The Arctic glaciers are melting. The majestic ice crowns of the sea are weakening each day. The ice sheets that were our

homes are melting each day. We have all lived there for so long, now our home is getting destroyed and the polar bears are all dying. We have witnessed the tragic end of many of the bears around us. We don't have enough food anymore and the people in the Arctic have evacuated. We feel helpless. Greenland is a beautiful country, but we fear that due to global warming, not only will our home be lost but so will the countries that surround the Arctic. The Oracle, who is our guardian and guide, predicted that we may not live till 2100. The Oracle also told one of our ancestors that when we leave the Earth, billions of lives will be lost too. We need to rescue our clan. Will you help us?" said Rahul, hanging his head in sorrow.

The Prime Minister was shaken considerably by this. "We will most certainly help. You can stay here," he said as he led the polar bears to a room.

Amar felt so relieved for the first time since their ordeal had begun. Rahul and Amar strolled around Nuuk City and glimpsed the Northern Lights.

The Northern Lights were a swirling light pattern across the sky. Red, purple, and blue streams of light flashed and twirled all around the sky – a friendly face in the alien land of humans. The humans viewed it as a matter of scientific interest, but the polar bears thought it to be their guiding star.

A RAY OF HOPE.

It calmed the polar bears and Amar felt as though they had achieved great heights. The lights put his worries to rest, knowing that the humans might do something to help them.

That night, Amar slept soundly but Rahul was wide awake with doubts nagging his mind.

Would the humans recognise their pain? Would they understand the problem? Would they stop doing what they were doing? Was the damage already done? What would it take to save the world?

Susie, Tarun, Ashish and so many other familiar faces swam before him as he fell asleep in exhaustion.

However, he did not have to worry.

He had spoken up. It would not be long before his voice was heard.

"One of the children in thy bloodline
will be the greatest saviour of nature in all time.
They'll risk their lives for a treasure
That holds no measure.
Sailing across the clear blue sky
Simply on a gay whim, their spirits high!
To find inner calling, despite beration;
Unflinching against the greater conflagration.
A world plundered by humans – What will they do?
Renew this periled world anew.
Touch the blackening sky from afar
To find the environmental lodestar.
Feel the cruel feats of man
Find solace within their plan.
Walk across accursed land,
Yet, beauty lies within hand.
Dabble with sciences old and new,
To save the Earth and give it her due."

CHAPTER

IX

Mission Future

The message sold like hotcakes.
People vow to help, whatever it takes.

The next day, television and radio channels all over the land were crammed with airtime of the conversation between the 'Polar Brothers' and the Parliament members. All the papers screamed about the plight of the polar bears and the causes of global warming.

The Prime Minister of Greenland contacted the **IPCC – The Intergovernmental Panel on Climate Change** – which is a United Nations body that studies the impact of climate change.

The government calculated the cost of changing all the technology and factories to eco-friendly and green machinery. When they added it up to the grand total, the price was quite huge indeed.

However, oil companies and leading corporations around the world objected. "**Climate change is merely a hoax!** This conspiracy has been created by those organisations that want to profit from us shutting down!" they fumed, referring to the statements made by a few scientists. "Where is the evidence that emissions create it? It could be caused by cosmic waves too. This is a baseless theory."

Data scientists, analysts and climatologists were consulted. The evidence was overwhelming. Yet, the Prime Minister decided that they would do a check to see the picture that the polar bears had predicted. After all, visualising an enemy before tackling it was just what was needed. Especially when handling the entire fate of the Earth.

A large and efficient Time Machine was being built just for the purpose of observing and analyzing the degree of damage done to the past and to see the outcome of climate change in the future. They prepared to assess what could be done to improve the present-day climate crisis.

Engineers and physicists did a few dry runs with it, and all the genius scientists of the past were brought to the present. They were assigned a mission of utmost importance. The scientists worked tirelessly in their labs.

With state-of-the-art technology, the Time Machine was crafted, and the scientists who had worked their way into history prepared to undertake the mission. From the unified field theory to the radioactive metals, from laws of physics to great mechanics, many great minds were brought together.

REAKING NEWS
GT
E 'POLAR BROTHERS' NLIGHTEN THE GOVT BOUT CLIMATE CRISIS
OIL COMPANIES
Climate change is merely a HOAX!
This is a baseless theory
Where is the evidence that emissions create it?
BUSINESS CORPORATIONS
ST OF CONVERTING TO ECO-FRIENDLY SYSTEMS
LABORATORY

Millions were donated for this mission and the work went on in full swing. Soon, they began setting up a huge terminal at the centre of Nuuk.

Across the world, many prayed for the mission's success.

After the Time Machine was built and several trials were run, the date was set, and everyone showed up to watch time travel for the first time in public.

"One of the children in thy bloodline
will be the greatest saviour of nature in all time.
They'll risk their lives for a treasure
That holds no measure.
Sailing across the clear blue sky
Simply on a gay whim, their spirits high!
To find inner calling, despite beration;
Unflinching against the greater conflagration.
A world plundered by humans – What will they do?
Renew this periled world anew.
Touch the blackening sky from afar
To find the environmental lodestar.
Feel the cruel feats of man
Find solace within their plan.
Walk across accursed land,
Yet, beauty lies within hand.
Dabble with sciences old and new,
To save the Earth and give it her due.
Greyer future, innocent past,
Watch habitable Earth breathe her last."

CHAPTER

X

The Time Machine

With a Time Machine, to the future they go
Get ready to face global warming, their foe.

On January 3, 2031, a countdown was initiated inside the spacious Time Machine, a purple and dark green whirring vehicle with room for more than 10 people. It had a dial to adjust the time to the scientists' will and a biometric pad to ensure proper authorisation for usage.

It also had emergency power and levers in case of an adverse event. It had been built over the course of several months, for times like this, and the greatest intellectuals had built it together. It was no ordinary feat and was nothing short of a turning point in history.

"15, 14, 13, 12, 11, 10, 9, 8, 7, 6, 5, 4, 3, 2,1, Energy sample

100% transmitted" came the voice of the AI controller.

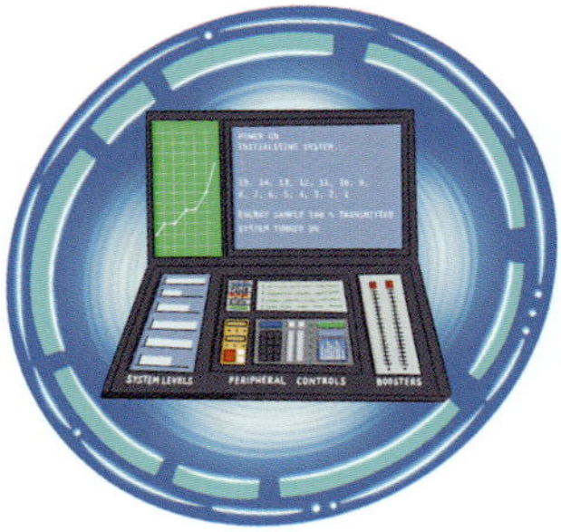

WOOOOOOOOOEEEEEEEE-BLAM!

A button appeared and when the engineer pressed it, the whole vehicle coursed with electricity of more than a million volts – it was almost like being inside a nuclear bomb that was ready to detonate due to the smallest of fluctuations.

The machine began its Artificial Intelligence programming with a bunch of click-clacks and a beeping sound in the background.

Flarie Turie pressed her palm against the machine and slowly turned the steering wheel clockwise. A dial showing the year 2031 appeared and she persisted until the dial read 2100.

Brilliant bursts of colour flashed through the machine, and suddenly, all was calm.

"One of the children in thy bloodline
will be the greatest saviour of nature in all time.
They'll risk their lives for a treasure
That holds no measure.
Sailing across the clear blue sky
Simply on a gay whim, their spirits high!
To find inner calling, despite beration;
Unflinching against the greater conflagration.
A world plundered by humans – What will they do?
Renew this periled world anew.
Touch the blackening sky from afar
To find the environmental lodestar.
Feel the cruel feats of man
Find solace within their plan.
Walk across accursed land,
Yet, beauty lies within hand.
Dabble with sciences old and new,
To save the Earth and give it her due.
Greyer future, innocent past,
Watch habitable Earth breathe her last.
Souls of the world, ripped apart
Can there be a greener start?"

CHAPTER XI

Time Travel To The Year 2100

2100 – a disastrous year for mankind
Severe catastrophe – they find.

In the year 2100, the crew in the Time Machine witnessed colossal damage due to global warming.

Half of the glaciers and polar caps had melted, increasing sea levels around the world by a shocking 25%.

The sky was burning red, and they were unable to step out of the Time Machine. The land was barren, the sea levels had risen by 12 feet and billions were at risk.

The global warming level had been increasing every day, and at that rate, it had become irreversible.

The rain came rarely, and even then, the sky had turned pale orange and dark from all the carbon emissions. The ground cracked in rage and acid flowed along with the precious drops of rain.

The sea levels were going to rise by 2000 metres by the end of this year. The world was exposed to fires, storms, droughts, and floods. The chance for survival was terribly low, and increased heart attacks, asthma, wheezing, eye issues, and irritations of the nose and throat were common everywhere.

Several places across the world were drowned by huge tides.

Many industries all over the world were closed and there was an economic meltdown.

Even worse, many species of animals had gone extinct or were poised for extinction.

Yet, many of the remaining factories puffed more and more smoke into the sky, which responded with torrents of lightning.

The human race was dying out – fast.

It seemed like the ultimate revenge of the Earth.

Flarie Turie pulled out a tab and swiped at it with a stylus.

“There is some severe damage done to places such as Lagos in Nigeria, Jakarta in Indonesia, New York in the USA, London in England, and several Indian cities like Mumbai, Chennai, Kochi, and Vishakhapatnam.

2100

Nearby areas also are affected," she said.

"Oh, I used to live near Chennai, in India," added SP Daman. "It is disheartening to witness this day!"

"We all worked so hard to make inventions for mankind, but we never imagined it would lead to this," said Zack Rewton sadly.

They were all horrified at the destruction that was unfolding before their eyes.

The Earth had been stripped of the green and blue. It was now black and red. Nature was seeking vengeance.

THE HUMAN RACE WAS DOOMED.

"One of the children in thy bloodline
will be the greatest saviour of nature in all time.
They'll risk their lives for a treasure
That holds no measure.
Sailing across the clear blue sky
Simply on a gay whim, their spirits high!
To find inner calling, despite beration;
Unflinching against the greater conflagration.
A world plundered by humans – What will they do?
Renew this periled world anew.
Touch the blackening sky from afar
To find the environmental lodestar.
Feel the cruel feats of man
Find solace within their plan.
Walk across accursed land,
Yet, beauty lies within hand.
Dabble with sciences old and new,
To save the Earth and give it her due.
Greyer future, innocent past,
Watch habitable Earth breathe her last.
Souls of the world, ripped apart
Can there be a greener start?
Dusk of the west, hope is curtailed,
***The desolate shores have been sailed.**"*

CHAPTER

XII

Year 463 In The Land Of Zephyros

Travel to 463 – the land of Zephyros
Where a tidal wave shows them who's boss.

Just then, the scientists noticed some beeps coming from the alarm of the Time Machine. The screen above the dial of the clock was showing the year 463.

The analysis given by the Time Machine reported a pattern of sea level increase and calamities in the year 463. There was notable seismic activity.

"There was no global warming in the year 463. Though global warming contributes majorly to sea level increase, there could have been other reasons too. There seems to have been some alarming landslides and seismic activity.

Let's pull in. What was the impact that year?" questioned Tephen Rawking.

Intrigued, the scientists selected the year on the dial as they had never thought that something similar had happened in the past too!

They wound the steering wheel on the Time Machine counterclockwise, and the machine began its whirring and beeping as bolts of energy and light surrounded it once again.

When it reached the year 463, they witnessed a heavenly scene. Things were so perfect, as though it was a Claude Monet painting.

They saw people selling fruit in loud voices at many stalls, and bartering goods. They were all very pleased.

The scientists realised that it was fine to step out now; there was no calamity here.

They stepped out of the Time Machine's elevator, where a carpet of purple and scarlet hibiscuses greeted them.

Ships arrived at the dock and people unloaded heavy crates of goods such as clay pots, mangoes, bananas, and other exotic fruits.

An old man with a toothy grin offered them some mangoes, which they accepted gratefully.

There was a clang as another ship entered the port and the crew brought out huge bundles of firewood and incense.

One man lit a fire by rubbing two sticks together and everyone gathered around it. The air smelled of petrichor and all was peaceful.

That's when a loud crack resounded through the streets. The people shuffled nervously. The world seemed to spin around them.

People at the seashore were seen running for their lives. In a moment, a tidal wave crashed upon all of them. There were loud shouts and yelling, and they all began running in different directions.

The scientists stared in horror as trees were uprooted, lightning flashed, thunder roared, and deadly arcs of water destroyed huts and washed people off their feet.

A bolt of lightning zapped at the nearest tree, setting it on fire and a gusty gale whooshed and hissed. An uprooted tree smashed the Time Machine. The electricity from the machine made it burst into flames and set the whole road on fire!

"Oh no! Quick, hoist up the machine!" said Tephen Rawking. They flung the door open and entered. The glass was cracked, the dial was popping out in an odd direction, and the lights and buttons were dark, except for a glowing lever. The label on it said 'Emergency Lever'. They reached for it just as a branch slammed against the elevator. Hard.

The automated voice groaned: **"Protective steel integrity - 31 %."** They grabbed the lever, pulled it down and the power came back.

A tidal wave crashed and smashed against the glass which gave way. The automated voice said: "Protective steel

ZEPHYROS

integrity 1%." Romus E Jedison activated the flight system and the whole machine jerked up high in the air.

There was stunned silence for five seconds.

Then, Lambert Reinsten said, **"Activate external UAV."** The droid, P320, used its external camera to transmit a map. They watched in shock, as the whole land of Zephyros sunk into a dot in the map and finally, disappeared.

The scientists gave a sad look at their memento from the Land of Zephyros – the ripe Alphonso mangoes offered to them by the generous old man.

How they wished they could take all the people from the fallen kingdom of Zephyros into the Time Machine and transport them to a secure future! But how did it sink so fast!

A few scientists looked at the maps of Zephyros and found that mining was extensively practised in several parts of the country. This not only caused pollution but also eroded the soil. This further led to turbulences in the tectonic plates that triggered earthquakes and tidal waves. The country sank into the sea. This was just the first disaster caused by humans and their squandering of resources.

Lambert Reinsten drew himself up and said -"We know that witnessing this is indeed sorrowful. However, we must work towards preventing such an incident in the future. Several disasters occur due to our squandering of environmental resources. We can stop these and work for the betterment of our climate."

The scientists slowly nodded their heads in agreement. "We must return and do something about this situation immediately," SP Daman declared.

"One of the children in thy bloodline
will be the greatest saviour of nature in all time.
They'll risk their lives for a treasure
That holds no measure.
Sailing across the clear blue sky
Simply on a gay whim, their spirits high!
To find inner calling, despite beration;
Unflinching against the greater conflagration.
A world plundered by humans – What will they do?
Renew this periled world anew.
Touch the blackening sky from afar
To find the environmental lodestar.
Feel the cruel feats of man
Find solace within their plan.
Walk across accursed land,
Yet, beauty lies within hand.
Dabble with sciences old and new,
To save the Earth and give it her due.
Greyer future, innocent past,
Watch habitable Earth breathe her last.
Souls of the world, ripped apart
Can there be a greener start?
Dusk of the west, hope is curtailed,
The desolate shores have been sailed.
Would there be any hope
Can planet liveable even cope?"

CHAPTER

XIII

The Time Is Now

Return to the future – protection's underway
To stop the Earth from turning grey.

Once the scientists returned to year 2031, they advised the government to convert to eco-friendly systems and protect nature to avoid the grim picture that the future had for them.

The World Climate Revolution was launched, the world's infrastructure was improved, and pollution levels dropped. A science committee was formed, and they all came up with methods to reduce pollution.

Electric cars, green electricity, and factories with windmills and solar panels were installed. Governments across the world took initiatives to reduce the use of fossil fuels.

SUSTAINABLE SYSTEMS FOR EARTH
WCR
Global warming could be tackled through basic ways & kids could contribute easily too
Vivvaan
ECO WARRIORS
ECO WARRIORS

The Greenland Base for Environmental Protection led the World Climate Revolution, which was backed, funded, and taken up in many countries.

It was headed towards making the world a better place.

A young environmentalist named Vivvaan Bajpayee, aged 18 years, started an initiative in India. He educated people regarding global warming and many people came together in his initiative to work for a better cause.

He gave thought provoking speeches in schools and in the media, and shared information on how global warming could also be tackled in basic ways, and how contributions could be made by kids too!

This encouraged all kids to be eco-warriors.

Meanwhile, in Greenland, the PM gave the details of the World Climate Revolution to Amar and Rahul and told them about the developments being made around the world.

Amar was delighted to hear this.

Despite these initiatives, there was a sense of dissatisfaction among the different groups of people. All the measures taken by the government were just slowing down the toll of global warming and climate change. While the enterprises felt that governments were being unfair to them, the common people felt that the government needed to enforce stricter rules on the factories.

Overall, what was lacking was self-realisation and self-motivation.

"One of the children in thy bloodline
will be the greatest saviour of nature in all time.
They'll risk their lives for a treasure
That holds no measure.
Sailing across the clear blue sky
Simply on a gay whim, their spirits high!
To find inner calling, despite beration;
Unflinching against the greater conflagration.
A world plundered by humans – What will they do?
Renew this periled world anew.
Touch the blackening sky from afar
To find the environmental lodestar.
Feel the cruel feats of man
Find solace within their plan.
Walk across accursed land,
Yet, beauty lies within hand.
Dabble with sciences old and new,
To save the Earth and give it her due.
Greyer future, innocent past,
Watch habitable Earth breathe her last.
Souls of the world, ripped apart
Can there be a greener start?
Dusk of the west, hope is curtailed,
The desolate shores have been sailed.
Would there be any hope
Can planet liveable even cope?
Gemstones moulded by helplessness and pain
Help the world recover, regain."

CHAPTER

XIV

The Time Machine Escapade

Pollution still done to the world of man
Then Rahul comes up with a genius plan.

In contrast to Amar's excitement, Rahul remained perturbed. He was troubled by how much pollution there was and how little these methods would resolve their problems.

One day, Amar and Rahul were lazing on Rocky Beach when they saw intense smoke in the sky. It rose and completely clogged up the sky. Soon, the wind blew, and the smoke was dispersed.

"It makes me feel so sad to see all this, Amar. The pollution spoils everything around it. The methods adopted by governments across the world are just postponing the effect of global warming.

Eventually, the vehicles and factories will produce so much smoke that the environment will be overwhelmed," Rahul said sadly.

Amar was greatly upset by this. "What if all these humans were not there to pollute so much? What if all these factories were not there? If the humans were not there, would we all be able to live properly?" he burst out indignantly.

That's when **RAHUL HAD A BRAINWAVE!**

"Follow me!" he said. Rahul clambered off the beach and began to run. Amar, not wanting to miss out on anything, ran after him.

They zig–zagged throughout the land, jumping, and leaping until they reached a large facility.

Amar stopped, caught his breath, and asked, "What are you doing?" Rahul's eyes just gleamed, and he pushed the door. The lock refused to open, so they climbed up the water pipes and reached the terrace. To their luck, someone had forgotten to lock the terrace door and they went inside the facility.

A huge hall stretched ahead of them. Then, they noticed a vault at the end of the corridor. It had a number lock on it. "We need to open this, and quick!" said Rahul.

After trying a few options, Amar recollected something he had overheard the scientists discussing. He entered – 7/11/67. It was Flarie Turie's birthday. The vault whirred and opened.

Amar gasped for breath as he gazed at what was securely stashed in the vault. He guessed what his brother was about to do!

"One of the children in thy bloodline
will be the greatest saviour of nature in all time.
They'll risk their lives for a treasure
That holds no measure.
Sailing across the clear blue sky
Simply on a gay whim, their spirits high!
To find inner calling, despite beration;
Unflinching against the greater conflagration.
A world plundered by humans – What will they do?
Renew this periled world anew.
Touch the blackening sky from afar
To find the environmental lodestar.
Feel the cruel feats of man
Find solace within their plan.
Walk across accursed land,
Yet, beauty lies within hand.
Dabble with sciences old and new,
To save the Earth and give it her due.
Greyer future, innocent past,
Watch habitable Earth breathe her last.
Souls of the world, ripped apart
Can there be a greener start?
Dusk of the west, hope is curtailed,
The desolate shores have been sailed.
Would there be any hope
Can planet liveable even cope?
Gemstones moulded by helplessness and pain
Help the world recover, regain.
A world without the sapiens story,
Is filled with bluer and greener glory."

CHAPTER

XV

The Legendary Discovery

There's no time to waste on talk
It's 2200 on the clock.

Are you sure about this?" asked Amar as they got into the Time Machine and launched the programming.

"Trust me. If everything goes according to my plan, I will make a breakthrough in history," said Rahul.

The Time Machine powered up, humming with energy. It glowed until it was white hot and **BOOM**!

The Time Machine was surrounded by dozens of blurry colours.

2200

Amar turned the steering wheel of the time controller and set it to 2100. They recorded the damage done in 2100 Earth and then Rahul turned the wheel to the year 2200.

Here, they stepped out to an astonishingly peaceful world. A few animals were grazing, and the air blew in gusts – a gentle breeze which calmed them.

However, there was not a single human in sight – no factories, no oil pumpers, no industry, no pollution. It was simply peaceful. They recorded all this and took the footage back with them.

Suddenly, the Time Machine juddered. The marker said: "The power is lost. Reserve power is critically low." The Time Machine left the alternative reality and took off.

They zipped back to the present year with the power fluctuating again and again. The booster rocket stopped working and rebooted. The machine AI rebooted and stopped. A static noise filled the machine. The terminals heated up and burst into flames.

The polar bears yelped and dodged the burning flames. The machine was so heated that it became difficult to stand on the floor.

The whole machine was going to crash! Below their feet, Rahul and Amar could see that the Time Machine was plummeting without control. Before it crashed, they leapt out of the Time Machine and jumped. They rolled and dived for cover, and the Time Machine crashed into the ground at a distance.

Rahul remembered to carry the footage as he jumped. They ran back to the remains of the machine and felt a pang of guilt. Little did they know that the machine had to be charged to full capacity before it was launched.

They watched the footage once more and yet again, the visuals reiterated that when the humans were not there, it was a peaceful world.

As they watched the Time Machine crumbling, they knew that they had to spread the message.

"One of the children in thy bloodline
will be the greatest saviour of nature in all time.
They'll risk their lives for a treasure
That holds no measure.
Sailing across the clear blue sky
Simply on a gay whim, their spirits high!
To find inner calling, despite beration;
Unflinching against the greater conflagration.
A world plundered by humans – What will they do?
Renew this periled world anew.
Touch the blackening sky from afar
To find the environmental lodestar.
Feel the cruel feats of man
Find solace within their plan.
Walk across accursed land,
Yet, beauty lies within hand.
Dabble with sciences old and new,
To save the Earth and give it her due.
Greyer future, innocent past,
Watch habitable Earth breathe her last.
Souls of the world, ripped apart
Can there be a greener start?
Dusk of the west, hope is curtailed,
The desolate shores have been sailed.
Would there be any hope
Can planet liveable even cope?
Gemstones moulded by helplessness and pain
Help the world recover, regain.
A world without the sapiens story,
Is filled with bluer and greener glory.
So, the eastern dawn can greet sunrise
Without any regret in its eyes."

CHAPTER

XVI

Spreading The Message

Give a speech to help the world repair
"The Earth needs humanity's care."

On March 13th, 2031, Rahul gathered a crowd of over a million people with Amar's help. He stood at the microphone, towering before all of them and began to speak.

"Nature is a gift. A gift constantly renewed by itself. Mountains, plateaus, icebergs, deserts, and such. These landforms make up nature, with at least 500,000 animals. These animals are dying out, Nature is crippled by constant attacks, driving the Earth barren to the core.

These fossil fuels burn in factories and produce greenhouse gases and pollutants which destroy the ozone layer. This is spoiling our environment.

We polar bears have seen the destruction inflicted by humans. We have watched, as the burning, summer sun has claimed all of our habitat and drilled this Earth hollow. The Arctic is becoming a vast expanse of sea, an uninhabitable one.

Homes are being lost to the crisis that many deny. Yet, when they deny, they dig two graves – one for all the animals and living creatures, including themselves, and the faith that a unified, clean and green Earth can thrive. The human race drives itself to extinction.

My younger brother Amar and I travelled to 2200 using a Time Machine created by scientists. Humans are extinct by then. However, nature flourishes when there are no factories, and no industries taking up the entire Earth's resources and minerals. While humans still stand, they must give back to the environment.

When we stand, my friends, we use this Earth. When you use thousands of gadgets in your day-to-day lives, you dig up the Earth to its core to satisfy your needs.

The Earth has enough resources to satisfy our needs, not our greed. However, there is time to change, you must amend your actions. Together, in perfect harmony, we can build a world perfect for us all, where there is no crisis. This opportunity will not last. We must to do what we can, while we can."

Rahul went on to share several facts and data that they had collected through their time travels. He gave voice to all the pain that was felt by the animals and plants living alongside the humans. Yet, with these words, a brighter future was in sight, a newer hope.

He continued, "We have been exploiting Mother Nature, yet she keeps giving back to us. She takes care of us. Should we not give back to her and take care of her as she has taken care of us?"

The roar of applause never seemed to die down. The world spun in front of the two polar bears. The butterflies in Rahul's tummy vanished instantly. He was waking up to a cause, a new future.

They had had to flee their home and were currently in safe hands. Yet, they had ensured that their home would be safe and secure in the future too. They had risked themselves for hundreds of others and they had succeeded.

The icing on the cake was that the next day, a ship full of polar bears was brought in from the Arctic. All their friends and family were rescued. They surrounded Rahul and Amar and cheered for them.

The destroyed Time Machine was rebuilt with the saved blueprints.

All the scientists were returned to their respective time periods, except for Tephen Rawking, Flarie Turie, and SP Daman, who were elected leaders of the science committee. The committee was now taken to the next level.

Money came rolling in, billions of it, to resolve problems the world had. The world seemed to be created anew. The plants rejuvenated the world. Since the humans knew their survival was on the line, they did the best they could. Emissions were reduced by stopping many factories. Scientists and corporations worked together for innovative methods of production.

Businesses were held accountable for the pollution and smoke they generated and were fined. Many homes turned to eco-friendly alternatives. Solar power and wind turbines were put to use in many areas across the world. Rainwater harvesting became mandatory.

The world awoke to the needs of sustainable mobility. Houses were constructed more strategically. People began walking, cycling or using the bus. Metros also came up.

Each person wanted to reduce their own carbon footprint. They all decided to fly lesser, use recycled material, give up plastic and choose electric vehicles or carpooling.

Apart from reducing their carbon footprint and the pollution they caused, they wanted to help improve things too! Van Mahotsav was taken as an example, and across the world, everyone planted trees on the sides of the road, in empty plots and in front of their homes to give guests a leafy greeting.

Solar and electric cars zoomed by without worrying much about the pollution they left behind. So much excavation was unnecessary now. Industries flourished and the environment flourished too.

The scale of these events was different this time. This revolutionised the whole world, starting from the young and how each of his or her actions affected the environment. This awareness made many sympathetic to the natural cause and everyone pledged to help.

The world calmed down and rose again, swelling with trees, plants, eco-friendly machinery, and the best investment of time and money: **Nature.**

However, the science committee realised that the past needed to be informed about the effects of pollution, too.

EPILOGUE

"One minute to destination," said Tephen Rawking.
They all watched as the years zipped by — **2027, 2026, 2025, 2024...**

The bell dinged. The clock settled at the dial labelled 2024.

The scientists of the world stepped out to an astonished audience.

"Welcome. We are from the year 2031," began Flarie Turie, and she briefed them about the Time Travel.

"There is a problem you'll face in the near future. There will be huge global warming disasters. Animals will be stranded. People will fall ill from the smoke. As we all know, the future can only be righted if the past too is changed," said SP Daman.

Tephen Rawking went on to share all the data that they had collected from the past and future. He summed it up for the crowd: "We advise you to be mindful and take initiatives for a greener world."

And he handed them a book.

Where is this book, you ask?

You have just finished reading it.

1776

Let us return to the story of Miko. He lived with his shattered mind, solving the puzzle in an endless line of kaizen.

Little by little, he solved everything. The world moved on. He didn't see his cubs grow up, yet his instinct told him that his future generations would lead their clan to the eventual glory the Oracle promised.

Then, fully revealed, as his mind was left to its own devices, he saw the Earth's cruel and grey fate.

His mind travelled to the infinite distances that he could not. His fragile being refrained from stepping out. Yet, he wept for the sorrow of the future. He sobbed for what the world itself did not.

He met Rahul and Amar. Not face to face, mind, but he watched their greater deeds, as they saved the world. He could see the events of the future, his mind's eye was endless.

His finite being was contained, yet he travelled across the seas and saw Rahul and Amar. Every hair, every thought, he could feel.

Then, the spinning fragments of memory returned to him. He closed his eyes with ecstasy and opened them once more.

When he did, he recited.

"One of the children in thy bloodline
will be the greatest saviour of nature in all time!
They'll risk their lives for a treasure
That holds no measure.
Sailing across the clear blue sky
Simply on a gay whim, their spirits high!
To find inner calling, despite beration;
Unflinching against the greater conflagration.
A world plundered by humans – What will they do?
Renew this periled world anew.
Touch the blackening sky from afar
To find the environmental lodestar.
Feel the cruel feats of man
Find solace within their plan;
Walk across accursed land,
Yet, beauty lies within hand.
Dabble with sciences old and new,
To save the Earth and give it her due.
Greyer future, innocent past,
Watch habitable Earth breathe her last.
Souls of the world, ripped apart
Can there be a greener start?
Dusk of the west, hope is curtailed,
The desolate shores have been sailed.
Would there be any hope
Can planet liveable even cope?
Gemstones moulded by helplessness and pain
Help the world recover, regain.
A world without the sapiens story,
Is filled with bluer and greener glory.
So, the eastern dawn can greet sunrise
Without any regret in its eyes."

Life would thrive, because of his descendants.

He stared across the horizon in joy.

And uttered the final words he would say. They summed up what his descendants would do.

"It has come true."

CLIMATE CHANGE

Some notes from aspiring environmentalist, Vivvaan Bajpayee:

Global warming is a crisis that's already unfolding around us. Greenhouse gases – pollutants and chemicals – have risen to the atmosphere and increased the temperature of our planet. They absorb sun rays and increase the temperature.

The heat has taken a toll on climatic conditions around the world. It has also melted the ice in the polar caps, resulting in the sea levels rising. This poses a threat to countries all over the world.

People say that trees can help. Yes, they can, but only to an extent. Each tree can only absorb up to 25 kg of carbon a year. Methane, nitrogen and fluorine also pollute.

Global warming occurs slowly, but billions are at risk. The most important part of stopping global warming is to get the next generation to step in and step up. As Dr APJ Abdul Kalam once said, 'Children are the future of the society.'

Many such agreements, like the Agreements at Kyoto, Paris and Montreal are a step towards the better. However, they are just the beginning. Change begins with the individual. Most of all, kids.

You might wonder if fighting such a problem is too much for kids to handle.

Well, my friends, there are some simple ways to deal with global warming.

- **Save electricity**: Electricity around the world is produced through burning coal and other harmful gases. While saving electricity, we can also prevent global warming.

- **Save water**: Water is a precious resource, and we must not waste it. Due to a lack of water in some places, icebergs are being blasted and towed to areas with less water. This impacts the habitat of seals, polar bears and penguins.

- **Cycle, Walk or Carpool**: Cycling is a very efficient manner of transport that does not pollute through carbon emissions. Walking does not pollute either and is a good exercise. We cannot stop people from using cars entirely. Hence, carpooling comes into play. Many people can use the same car to get to a destination without wasting much fuel and polluting so much.

- **Increasing Public Transport**: This is also a good idea as public transport can take a large number of people in just one vehicle. It discourages people from using just cars and other private transport.

- **Conserve fuel**: We have to excavate lots of minerals to produce enough fuel for buses, cars, trucks, trains, ships, planes, bikes, etc. We must follow the green methods of transportation given above when we can.

- **Use less paper**: Using less paper means lesser number of trees will be chopped down. Trees take in carbon dioxide – the root cause of global warming along with other greenhouse gases – and release oxygen.

FACTS ABOUT CLIMATE CHANGE

The concentration of carbon dioxide, methane and nitrous oxide has not been so high in the last 800,000 years.

99% of Costa Rica's energy is taken from renewable sources. This energy is accessible to everyone in the country.

Greenland has the least amount of air pollution in the world.

In 2019, Moroccan officials declared one of their villages to be fully powered by solar energy!

Due to the hunger, sickness and weather disasters caused by climate change, 3,15,000 people die each year.

35% of species on land will go extinct due to climate change by 2050 if we continue with our current level of emissions.

If emissions are not cut down by 2030, climate change could become irreversible.

36 billion tons of CO2 are released each year.

Amongst the highest polluting countries, India is third after China and the USA.

Countries like Japan, Korea, Finland, Brazil and

Switzerland use sustainable transport – walking, cycling, public transport and bullet train. 77 % of travel in Finland is on foot!

Some countries have even invented electric planes.

Data hubs, flights and computers make up the majority of our carbon footprint.

Sea ice is not just a habitat, it also reflects away the sun's rays, making the planet cooler. When sea ice melts away, the planet begins to absorb more heat.

Climate change affects us by impacting our health. It also affects our jobs and causes drought. It leaves us with lesser area for habitation.

If the world's temperature increases by 2 degrees Celsius, then every 10 years, the Arctic will be free of ice.

Heat waves due to global warming can lead to 5 million deaths globally.

Nuclear energy, solar power, tidal and hydroelectric power, wind turbines and natural gas are a few eco-friendly alternatives for coal and fuel.

Eating meat can also greatly contribute to our carbon footprint. 15 % of emissions are caused by rearing livestock and farming. A single cow eructates up to 120 kg of methane per year. It can produce 2000 kg of methane in its lifetime. Cattle release 100 billion kg of methane a year. This causes 15 % of our emissions. Methane absorbs more heat than carbon!!

You can reduce your personal carbon footprint by avoiding flying, using sustainable mobility, using clean energy and eating less meat.

Footballer Lesein Mutunkei started the Trees4Goals challenge, where he planted a tree for every goal he scored. In this way, he followed his passion and fought deforestation.

Greta Thunberg started the "Fridays for Future" movement, where school children would skip classes on Friday and campaign for a better environment.

Initiatives taken up by countries around the world

India – National Mission for Enhanced Energy Efficiency
National Mission for a Green India
National Mission on Strategic Knowledge for Climate Change

USA – Inflation Reduction Act
National Climate Task Force

China – China's National Climate Change Programme

Japan – Green Growth Strategy
Climate Change Adaptation Act

Korea – Framework Act on Low Carbon, Green Growth
Carbon Neutral Green Growth Framework Act

Russia – Russian National Adaptation Plan

ACKNOWLEDGEMENTS

In my Arctic, I must say thank you to the many other polar bears around me who have helped me grow.

My parents, the Susie and Miko of my family, who motivated me to write.

My brother, Amar, who wanted a story about polar bears on ships, trains and cars, traveling till they reached their destination. I still remember writing the first of many drafts that day.

My teachers and mentors, the polar bear clan, who nurtured me in my writing path.

Sowmya Ma'am, the Marie Curie, whose radioactive power kindled the flames of this book.

Bhavana ma'am, who lit up this book with the vivid illustrations.

Bookosmia Team who let the Northern Lights of this book shine gorgeous across the horizon.

And myself, Rahul, I need to keep writing more. Not for all those around, but for myself.

ABOUT THE AUTHOR

Vivvaan Bajpayee lives with his parents and little brother in Bangalore and studies at National Public School, HSR, Bangalore. He is an avid reader and blogger. He passionately reads and reviews works of literature on social media and feels drawn to Green Literature. When he is not in school attending a lecture, he can be seen daydreaming about stories, and characters and penning stories and poems.

He loves to cycle around and play basketball, badminton, and chess. He can be often seen strumming his favourite tunes on his guitar.

When he grows up, he wants to become an author and an environmentalist. His first book 'Swarg Lok Park', emphasizes the role and responsibility of kids towards the environment. He is also one of the winners of 'CBSE Budding Authors Programme-2022' for his story 'The Day the Tap Ran Dry', which has been published on the Story Weaver platform.

A few of his poems and his story 'Save the Earth' have been published in the 'The Hindu Young World' magazine.

ABOUT THE ILLUSTRATOR

Bhavana is an illustrator and visual artist based in Bangalore. She holds a Master's degree in Visual Communication from Srishti Manipal Institute of Art, Design and Technology, Bangalore. She is passionate about stories and loves illustrating them especially for children. Apart from drawing, coffee, cats and music are things she can never say "no" to.

Imagine yourself travelling 100 years into the future. What is the world you would love to see?

I'M ______________________________

AND THIS IS HOW I CARE!

Things I do that make an Impact towards my Environment

AT HOME	AT SCHOOL